# Creepy Creatures

# Ladybirds

Monica Hughes

Heinemann
LIBRARY

Little Nippers

**www.heinemann.co.uk/library**
Visit our website to find out more information about **Heinemann Library** books.

To order:
☎ Phone 44 (0) 1865 888066
▤ Send a fax to 44 (0) 1865 314091
💻 Visit the Heinemann Bookshop at www.heinemann.co.uk/library to browse our catalogue and order online.

First published in Great Britain by Heinemann Library, Halley Court, Jordan Hill, Oxford OX2 8EJ, part of Harcourt Education. Heinemann is a registered trademark of Harcourt Education Ltd.

Designed by Jo Hinton-Malivoire and bigtop, Bicester
Models made by Jo Brooker
Originated by Dot Gradations
Printed by South China Printing Company, Hong Kong/China

ISBN 0 431 16302 2  (hardback)
06 05 04 03 02
10 9 8 7 6 5 4 3 2 1

ISBN 0 431 16307 3  (paperback)
06 05 04 03 02
10 9 8 7 6 5 4 3 2 1

**British Library Cataloguing in Publication Data**
Hughes, Monica
    Ladybirds. - (Creepy creatures)
    1.Ladybirds - Pictorial works - Juvenile literature
    I.Title
    595.7'69

**Acknowledgements**
The Publishers would like to thank the following for permission to reproduce photographs:
Ardea: Steve Hopkin pp8, 15, 20, John Mason p16, Alan Weaving pp22a & b; BBC NHU: Dietmar Nill pp14, 22a; Bruce Coleman: p9, Liz Eddison p6, Orion Press p22c, Kim Taylor p17; NHPA: Stephen Dalton p7, Martin Garwood pp4/5; Oxford Scientific Films: Paulo D Oliveira pp11, 12, Herbert Schwind/Okapia, p13; Premaphotos: K Preston-Mapham, p21; Science Photo Library: Claude Nuridsany & Marie Perennou, pp10, 18.

Cover photograph reproduced with permission of Bruce Coleman Collection/ Robert Maier.

Our thanks to Annie Davy for help in the preparation of this book.

Every effort has been made to contact copyright holders of any material reproduced in this book. Any omissions will be rectified in subsequent printings if notice is given to the Publisher.

# Contents

# Ladybirds

Do you know what a ladybird looks like? Ladybirds are small beetles.

Most ladybirds are red with black spots.

# Looking for ladybirds

You can look for ladybirds in parks and gardens.

They are
easy to find
in summer.

# A ladybird's body

Ladybirds are insects. Their bodies have three parts.

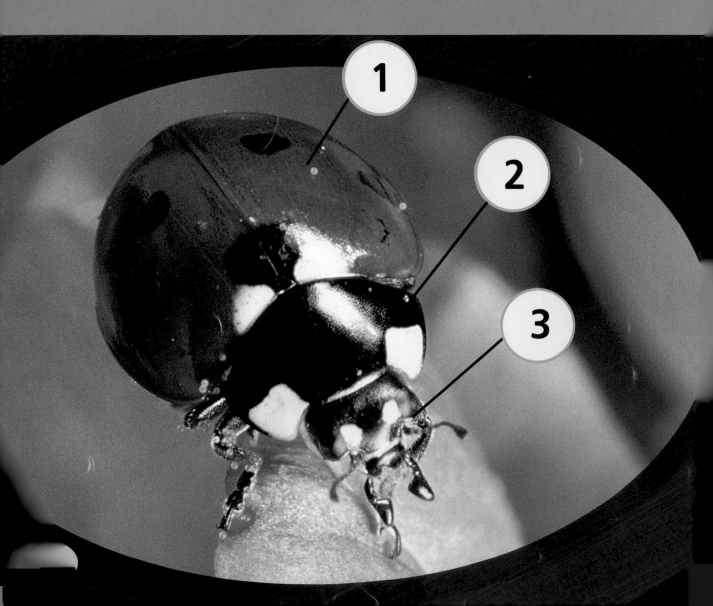

antenna

leg

They have six
**black** legs and
two **hairy** antennae.

# A ladybird's wings

Ladybirds have two pairs of wings.

You can only see the
large wings when a
ladybird is flying.

# Ladybird eggs

The female ladybird
lays lots of little eggs.

A larva hatches out of the eggs after about four days.

# Larva to pupa

The tiny larva eats and eats and grows and grows and **grows.**

After about three weeks
the larva changes into
a pupa.

# Young ladybirds

A young ladybird comes out of the pupa after about a week.

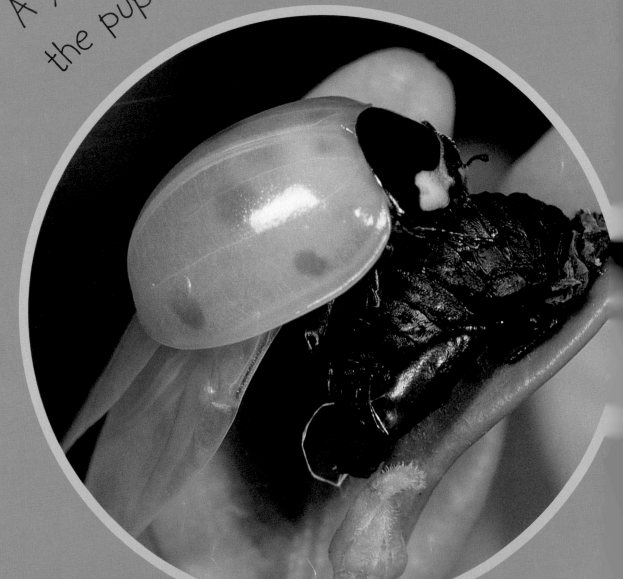

Young ladybirds are yellow.

17

# Food for ladybirds

Ladybirds eat tiny insects called aphids. Can you see the aphids?

# Ladybirds in danger

Ants attack ladybirds because they want to eat the aphids too.

When a ladybird is in danger
it will squirt a nasty poison.

squirt

# Types of ladybirds

There are thousands of different types of ladybirds.

# Index

The end

## Notes for adults

This series supports the young child's exploration of their learning environment and their knowledge and understanding of their world. The four books when used together will enable comparison of similarities and differences to be made. (NB. Many of the photographs in **Creepy Creatures** show them much larger than life size) The first spread of each title shows the creature at approximately its real life size.) The following Early Learning Goals are relevant to the series:
• Find out about, and identify, some features of living things, objects and events that they observe.
• Ask questions about why things happen and how things work.
• Observe, find out about and identify features in the place they live and the natural world.
• Find out about their local environment and talk about those features they like and dislike.

The books will help the child to extend their vocabulary, as they will hear new words. Some of the words that may be new to them in **Ladybirds** are *insect, beetle, larva, pupa, hatches, aphids* and *antennae*. Since words are used in context in the book this should enable the young child to gradually incorporate them into their own vocabulary.

### The following additional information may be of interest:
Ladybirds are insects as they have six legs and a body divided into three parts. They are members of the beetle family. Unlike the other creatures in the series the ladybird has a complex life cycle from egg to adult. Ladybirds cannot hear but can feel vibrations with their feet. The larvae are blind. Very few creatures attack ladybirds, as their bright colour is a warning that they do not taste very nice. They are also able to squirt a bitter liquid at an attacker. Ladybirds are popular with farmers and gardeners as they eat the pests that destroy flowers and crops.

### Follow-up activities
The child can record what they have found out about ladybirds – especially their life cycle – by drawing, painting and writing. Also relate factual information about ladybirds to traditional rhymes like *Ladybird, Ladybird, fly away home*, and stories such as *The Bad Tempered Ladybird* by Eric Carle.